DOMINOES

Sheherazade

STARTER LEVEL   250 HEADWORDS

OXFORD
UNIVERSITY PRESS

Great Clarendon Street, Oxford OX2 6DP

Oxford University Press is a department of the University of Oxford.
It furthers the University's objective of excellence in research, scholarship,
and education by publishing worldwide in

Oxford New York

Auckland Cape Town Dar es Salaam Hong Kong Karachi
Kuala Lumpur Madrid Melbourne Mexico City Nairobi
New Delhi Shanghai Taipei Toronto

With offices in

Argentina Austria Brazil Chile Czech Republic France Greece
Guatemala Hungary Italy Japan Poland Portugal Singapore
South Korea Switzerland Thailand Turkey Ukraine Vietnam

OXFORD and OXFORD ENGLISH are registered trade marks of
Oxford University Press in the UK and in certain other countries

This edition © Oxford University Press 2011

The moral rights of the author have been asserted

Database right Oxford University Press (maker)

2015 2014 2013 2012 2011

10 9 8 7 6 5 4 3 2 1

ISBN: 978 0 19 424716 0   Book
ISBN: 978 0 19 424680 4   Book and MultiROM Pack

MultiROM not available separately

Printed in China

This book is printed on paper from certified and well-managed sources.

ACKNOWLEDGEMENTS

*The publisher would like to thank the following for their kind permission to reproduce photographs and
other copyright material*: Alamy pp.30 (Sultan Hassan Mosque, Cairo/imagebroker), 43 (The
Registan, Uzbekistan/Jon Arnold), 43 (Historical building, Basra, Iraq/Images&Stories),
43 (Cairo/World Religions Photo Library), 44 (Lake Lucerne/F1online digitale Bildagentur
GmbH), 44 (Windmills,La Mancha/Michelle Chaplow), 44 (Sherwood Forest/Arterra Picture
Library), 44 (Sherwood Forest/Greg Balfour Evans); Getty pp.19 (Mongolian polo players/
Michel Setboun), 44 (Bedouin tents/Thomas J. Abercrombie/National Geographic); Royal
Shakespeare Company pp.40 (Arabian nights/The little beggar/Keith Pattison © Royal
Shakespeare), 41 (Arabian nights/The 40 Thieves/Keith Pattison © Royal Shakespeare).

Illustrations by: Laure Fournier (All story pages); Fred Van Deelen pp.42 (The Silk Road map), 43.

Cover image: Laure Fournier

DOMINOES

Series Editors: Bill Bowler and Sue Parminter

Sheherazade

Retold by Bill Bowler

Illustrated by Laure Fournier

Bill Bowler studied English Literature at Cambridge University and mime in Paris before becoming an English language teacher, trainer, and materials writer. He loves the theatre, opera, ballet, cinema, history, art, storytelling – and travelling. He also enjoys reading books and writing poetry in his free time. Bill lives in Alicante with his wife, Sue Parminter, and their three children. This Dominoes retelling of the *Sheherazade* story is based on many different versions of the *Thousand and One Nights* tale.

OXFORD
UNIVERSITY PRESS

BEFORE READING

1 This is Sheherazade. What do you know about her? Tick the boxes.

		True	False
a	She's from Egypt.	☐	☐
b	She lives in a palace.	☐	☐
c	She's got a younger sister.	☐	☐
d	Her father is a king.	☐	☐
e	She likes listening to stories.	☐	☐
f	She likes telling stories.	☐	☐

2 What things do the people in Sheherazade's stories do? Match every person with what they do. Use a dictionary to help you.

a A little beggar

b A doctor

c A poor man from Baghdad

d An old man from India

1 ... kills a king.

2 ... gives a flying black horse to a king.

3 ... eats a fish and nearly dies.

4 ... finds a lot of treasure near his house.

~ CHAPTER 1 ~
Kings and their wives

One day Shahriyar, **King** of Indochina, writes to his brother, Shahzaman, King of Samarkand.

Soon after he reads this, Shahzaman is ready to leave. But at the **palace** door he stops.

'My brother's **present**! It's in my room!' he cries.

He runs back for it, and finds his **wife** there, with one of his **servants**.

'When Shahzaman dies, you can be king,' she says to the young man.

'I'm away for only five minutes and look!' thinks Shahzaman, angrily. 'I can never **trust** my wife again!'

So he **cuts off** the man's head and his wife's head with his **sword**. Then he takes the present, and leaves.

king the most important man in a country

palace a big house where a king lives

present something that you give to someone

wife a woman living with a man

servant a person who works for someone rich

trust to believe that someone is nice and good

cut off to take a smaller thing from a bigger thing with a knife

sword a long sharp knife for fighting

1

In Indochina, Shahzaman gives the present to his brother without a smile. Shahriyar asks, 'What's the matter?'

'I can't say,' answers Shahzaman. 'But something's badly wrong.'

'Forget it, and come **hunting**!' says Shahriyar.

'Not today!' says Shahzaman.

So Shahriyar leaves for the hunt and Shahzaman stays in his room. Later, from his window, he sees Shahriyar's wife and twenty of her women by the **pool** in the garden. With them are twenty-one servants – tall, dark young men with big smiles.

'My brother's wife is many times worse than my wife!' thinks Shahzaman.

hunt to look for and kill animals; when you look for and kill animals

pool water in a garden

That night, when Shahriyar comes home, Shahzaman speaks about his wife and the servant in Samarkand.

'But, brother, why are you telling me this now?' asks Shahriyar.

So Shahzaman tells Shahriyar all about *his* wife, her women, and the servants by the pool.

'Not *my* wife, too!' cries Shahriyar. 'It isn't true!'

'Listen, brother,' says Shahzaman. 'Tomorrow your friends can go hunting without you. You can stay with me and see.'

So next morning Shahriyar watches through the window of Shahzaman's room. Soon his wife, her women, and the servants arrive by the pool.

'Massood,' Shahriyar's wife tells the young man by her, 'when Shahriyar is dead, you can be king.'

Shahriyar angrily calls six of his best men to him. 'Kill my wife, her women, and the servants by the pool!' he says. They do it at once.

After Shahzaman goes home, Shahriyar is not happy. He cannot stop loving women, but he cannot trust them.

Every afternoon he **marries** a new young wife, but the next morning he always tells the palace **executioner**, 'Cut off her head!'

His wives have no time to be bad.

But after some months, Shahriyar's **Vizier** cannot find any more wives.

'What can I do?' the Vizier cries. 'I don't want the executioner at my door tomorrow.'

When the Vizier arrives home that night, he isn't happy. His two daughters go to him. The older daughter is Sheherazade; her younger sister is Dunyazid.

'What's the matter, Father?' asks Sheherazade, and the Vizier tells her.

'But *I* can be Shahriyar's new wife!' says Sheherazade. '**God willing** I can stay alive, and help the women of our country, too.'

'Sheherazade, no!'

'Father, take me to the King,' says Sheherazade.

In the end, the Vizier says 'Yes'.

marry to make someone your wife or husband

executioner this man works for the king and kills bad people for him

vizier an important man in an Arab country who helps the king

God willing if the important being who never dies, and who decides what happens in the world, wants it

Before Sheherazade leaves, she tells Dunyazid, 'Come to me tonight when I call, and ask for a story. God willing, that can help us.'

Then the Vizier takes Sheherazade to the King, and Shahriyar marries her.

That night, in the King's room, Sheherazade says, 'My King, I want to say goodbye to my young sister. Can I call her here?'

'Of course,' says the King.

After they say their goodbyes, Dunyazid smiles, 'Sister, your stories always help the long, dark night hours to go quickly. Can you tell me one last story tonight?'

'Can I, my King?' Sheherazade asks.

'You can,' answers Shahriyar. 'I love a good story.'

So Sheherazade begins:

*In Basra a **tailor** lives with his wife. They're good people. One evening, they meet a little **beggar** in the street. He's drinking, telling stories and laughing, and the tailor and his wife laugh with him.*

'Come home with us for something to eat,' they say.

tailor a man who makes coats, trousers and other things to wear

beggar a person who asks other people for money in the street

READING CHECK

Match the sentence halves.

a Shahzaman goes to Indochina
b Before he leaves his palace, he kills his wife
c Shahriyar sees his wife with a young man
d After this, he marries many women,
e One day, Shahriyar's Vizier
f He goes home and speaks to
g His older daughter, Sheherazade,
h That night, Dunyazid asks Sheherazade,

1 and kills her too.
2 cannot find any more wives for the king.
3 because he finds her with a young man.
4 and visits his brother, Shahriyar, there.
5 but he kills them all after one night.
6 'Can you tell me one last story?'
7 his two daughters.
8 wants to marry Shahriyar.

WORD WORK

1 Complete the words from Chapter 1 to match the pictures.

a b̲e̲g̲g̲a̲r̲   b _ o _ _   c _ _ o _ _   d _ i _ _

e _ a _ a _ e   f _ a _ _ o _   g e _ _ _ u _ i _ _ e

2 Find six more words from Chapter 1 in the sword.

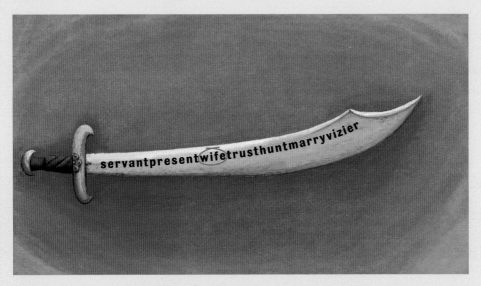

servantpresentwifetrusthuntmarryvizier

3 Use the words from Activity 2 to complete the sentences.

a Shahzaman cuts off his ..... wife ...... 's head because he is angy with her.

b The .... is an important man in the palace.

c Shahriyar does not .... women because of his first wife.

d The .... s do all the work in the palace.

e Shahriyar likes .... ing and killing things.

f Shahzaman gives his brother a .... from Samarkand.

g Sheherazade wants to .... Shahriyar and help her father.

GUESS WHAT

What happens in Chapter 2? Tick the boxes.

		Yes	No
a	Sheherazade finishes her story that night.	☐	☐
b	Sheherazade begins a new story in the early morning.	☐	☐
c	King Shahriyar finds the story interesting.	☐	☐
d	The executioner is waiting to kill Sheherazade.	☐	☐
e	The executioner kills Dunyazid.	☐	☐

~ **CHAPTER 2** ~
The little beggar

'Interesting!' says King Shahriyar. Dunyazid is interested, too, and Sheherazade **goes on** with the story:

go on not to stop

fish an animal that lives in water

bone a hard white thing in an animal's body

throat the inside of your neck

fall to go down suddenly; when you go down suddenly

blanket you put this over you when you sleep on a bed

*So the little beggar goes home with the tailor and his wife, and they have bread and **fish** to eat. Suddenly, when he's eating and laughing at the same time, the little beggar gets a fish **bone** in his **throat**. His face goes blue, and he **falls** from the table. His eyes close.*

'Get up, friend,' laughs the tailor. But the little beggar doesn't move. The tailor looks at him carefully.

'Oh, no!' he cries. 'Our little friend's dead! And we're his killers. What can we do?'

*'Put him in a **blanket**!' says his wife.*

So they put the little beggar in a blanket, and they take him out into the street.

*'Help! Our young child's ill!' cries the tailor's wife. 'Where's the nearest **doctor**?'*

At the doctor's front door, they tell the servant girl, 'Our child needs the doctor.'

*The girl goes to find the doctor, and the tailor and his wife stand the little beggar's body at the foot of the **stairs**. Then they run away back to their house.*

*The doctor runs down the stairs. In the dark he **knocks over** the beggar, and the little man falls at his feet. The doctor looks at him carefully.*

'Oh, no! This man's dead from the fall, and I'm his killer!' the doctor cries. 'What can I do?'

*'Quick!' says his wife. 'Let's move the body to our **neighbour's** house.'*

*So they take the body and stand it in the neighbour's **kitchen**.*

*Their neighbour is a **cook** at the palace. Every night he brings home good things to eat from the palace, but the neighbours' dogs and cats always come and eat them.*

doctor a person who helps people when they are ill

stairs you can go up or down these in a house

knock over to hit someone and make them fall

neighbour a person who lives near you

kitchen the room in a house where people make things to eat

cook a person who makes things for people to eat

9

When the cook comes home that night, he sees the little beggar in his dark kitchen. 'Aha! So the neighbours' cats and dogs aren't eating everything here. A man's doing it — and tonight I've got him!'

So the cook hits the little beggar again and again. The little beggar falls at his feet, and the cook looks at him carefully.

'Help! He's dead, and I'm his killer!' the cook cries. 'I must "lose" the body fast.'

So the cook takes the little beggar's body into the dark street and stands it by a shop.

Not long after that, a **rich** man goes and stands near the shop. Suddenly he sees the little beggar next to him in the dark street, and he feels afraid.

'Help! **Watchman**! This man wants to take my money from me!' he cries, and he hits the little beggar again and again. The little beggar falls at his feet.

rich with a lot of money

watchman a man who finds people that do bad things in the street

Suddenly, the watchman arrives. He sees the beggar at the rich man's feet, and he looks at the little man carefully.

'This man's dead, and you're his killer!' the watchman cries. 'Come with me.'

*The watchman takes the man to the **judge**, and all the neighbours come out of their houses and watch.*

The judge listens to the rich man and the watchman. He looks at the little beggar's body carefully. Then he says…

Just then, Sheherazade stops speaking.

'What's the matter with you, wife?' asks King Shahriyar.

'Look, my King,' says Sheherazade. She **points** to the red morning sky through the window. 'A new day is here. I cannot tell you more.'

Dunyazid cries.

Just then, the Vizier – Sheherazade's father – comes into the room.

'King Shahriyar,' he says, 'The executioner's waiting for your wife.'

Sheherazade gets up. 'Then take me to him, Father,' she says. 'I'm ready to die.'

READING CHECK

Choose the correct words to complete the sentences.

a 'The little beggar is _bad / ~~dead~~_!' the tailor and his wife think.

b They leave the beggar in a _teacher's / doctor's_ house.

c 'I'm this man's _friend / killer_ !' the doctor thinks.

d The doctor takes the beggar to a neighbour's _garden / kitchen_ .

e 'This man is _eating / drinking_ things here!' the cook thinks.

f The rich man sees the beggar near _his house / a shop_ .

g 'This rich man is the _beggar's / doctor's_ killer!' the watchman thinks.

h Sheherazade stops telling the story when she sees _her father / the morning sky_.

WORD WORK

1 The words don't match the pictures. Correct them.

a

blanket
.....~~bone~~.....

b

....blanket....

c

.....cook.....

d

..watchman..

e

....kitchen....

f

.....judge.....

g

....throat....

h

.....stairs.....

2 Use the words in the fish bones to complete the sentences.

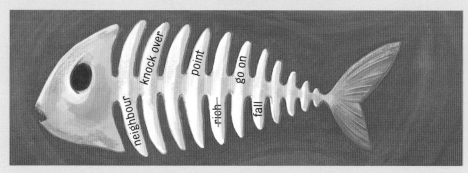

a The king has got a lot of money. He's very ......rich.......

b 'Look!' she says, and she ....s at some beautiful flowers.

c 'Please .... with the story. I'm interested,' says Shahriyar.

d 'I'm up in this tree. Please help me if I .... down.'

e 'That man lives in my street. He's my ....'

f 'Be careful! Don't .... that open bottle of water.'

GUESS WHAT

What do they do in the next chapter? Read and tick.

a

... tells the executioner:

1 ☐ 'Come back tomorrow morning!'

2 ☐ 'Kill Sheherazade now!'

3 ☐ 'Kill the Vizier now!'

b

1 ☐ ... dies the next morning.

2 ☐ ... never finishes the *Little Beggar* story.

3 ☐ ... begins a new story about a doctor.

c

1 ☐ ... dies the next morning.

2 ☐ ... goes and lives at the palace.

3 ☐ ... sits up and laughs at the judge.

Sheherazade is leaving the room with her father.

'Stop!' cries King Shahriyar. 'What happens to the rich man? I must know!'

'My King,' says Sheherazade. 'I can finish the story tonight. Do you want to hear it?'

'Yes!' cries Shahriyar, and to the Vizier he says, 'I don't need the executioner now. Call him tomorrow morning at this hour.'

So that night, Dunyazid comes again to the King's room, and Sheherazade goes on with her story:

Then the judge says, 'Call the executioner! This rich man is a killer and he must die.'

Just then, the cook cries, 'Wait! I'm the killer.' And he tells his story about the man in his kitchen.

'So the cook must die,' says the judge.

Suddenly, the doctor cries, 'No! I'm the killer.' And he tells the judge about the man at the foot of his stairs.

'Then the doctor must die,' says the judge.

At that, the tailor and his wife cry, 'Stop! We're the killers.' And they tell their story about the little beggar and the fish bone.

'So the tailor and his wife must die,' says the judge.

Just then, the fish bone falls out of the little beggar's mouth and he sits up, alive and well.

So in the end, nobody dies; and the little beggar goes and lives at the palace, because the King there loves good stories.

'Very good!' laughs King Shahriyar. 'But now you must die, Sheherazade. I'm sorry.'

Dunyazid cries, but Sheherazade isn't afraid. She points to the night sky through the window, and says, 'My King, there are many hours before morning. Would you like to hear a new story?'

'Yes!' says Shahriyar.

So Sheherazade begins:

King Yunan of Persia works every day for the good of his people. When he isn't working, he plays **polo**. *But he isn't happy, because he's badly ill with* **leprosy**. *Many doctors give different* **medicines** *to him. But nobody can* **cure** *him.*

Then one day, Duban the Doctor comes from far away and tells the King, 'I can cure you differently from the doctors here.'

'Do that, and you can be rich, and my best friend,' says King Yunan.

So Duban makes some medicine and puts it in a polo **stick**.

polo a game, like football, where people ride horses and hit a ball with a stick

leprosy when you have this illness, it can eat away your face and other body parts

medicine something that you eat or drink to help you get better when you are ill

cure to make an ill person better; something that makes someone who is ill better

stick a long, thin piece of wood

16

The next morning he tells Yunan, 'Take this stick, and go and play polo. With the stick in your warm hand for many hours, the medicine in it can go through your **skin** and cure you. After you finish playing, sit in a hot pool, and then go to bed. Do all this, and tomorrow you can get up a well man.'

King Yunan does it all, and the leprosy leaves his body the next day.

Happily, the King gives Duban lots of money, and says, 'From today, my friend, you must always sit by me.'

The next day, the Vizier – a bad man with a black **heart** – asks the King, 'Do you trust Duban?'

'Of course,' answers Yunan.

'Be careful,' says the Vizier. 'When a man can cure leprosy with medicine in a polo stick, he can easily put **poison** on something and kill you too.'

'Not good old Duban,' says Yunan.

But day after day, the Vizier says bad things about Duban, and one day…

Just then, Sheherazade's father – the Vizier – arrives.

'King Shahriyar,' he says. 'The executioner's waiting.'

skin what is on the outside of a person's body

heart the centre of feeling in somebody

poison something that kills people when they eat or drink it

ACTIVITIES

READING CHECK

Correct the mistakes in the sentences.

a First the judge says, 'The ~~poor~~ _rich_ man must die.'

b Then the cook cries, 'I'm the judge.'

c After that, the tailor and his wife tell the story of the fish head.

d Then the bone falls out of the little beggar's hand.

e In the end, the little beggar goes and lives with the doctor.

f Sheherazade sees the morning sky through the window.

g Her next story is about the King of Persia. He's very happy.

h One day a judge comes to Yunan's palace from far away.

i Duban's medicine makes the Vizier well again.

j Yunan's cook says bad things about Duban.

WORD WORK

1 Find seven more words from Chapter 3 in the wordsquare.

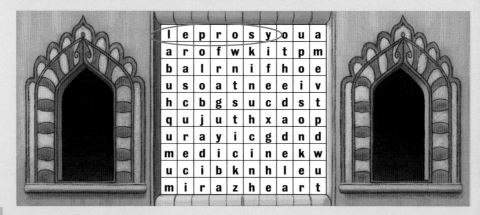

l	e	p	r	o	s	y	o	u	a
a	r	o	f	w	k	i	t	p	m
b	a	l	r	n	i	f	h	o	e
u	s	o	a	t	n	e	e	i	v
h	c	b	g	s	u	c	d	s	t
q	u	j	u	t	h	x	a	o	p
u	r	a	y	i	c	g	d	n	d
m	e	d	i	c	i	n	e	k	w
u	c	i	b	k	n	h	l	e	u
m	i	r	a	z	h	e	a	r	t

2 Use the words from Activity 1 to complete the sentences.

a There are people with ... leprosy ... in some countries today.

b The Vizier doesn't have a good .... He's a bad man.

c Doctor, please give me some .... I don't feel very well.

d When you play ...., you need a fast horse.

e My .... goes red when I sit in the sun for a long time.

f My grandfather can't walk without a ....·

g Doctor, can you .... my son? He's very ill.

h Stop! Don't drink from that cup. There's .... in it!

GUESS WHAT

What happens in the next chapter? Tick three sentences.

a The executioner kills Sheherazade and Dunyazid.

b Sheherazade finishes the story about Duban the Doctor.

c King Yunan's executioner cuts Duban in half.

d Duban doesn't die, and he kills Yunan with his sword.

e After Duban dies, he kills King Yunan with some poison.

f Sheherazade begins a new story before morning comes.

~ CHAPTER 4 ~
Dreams of far-away treasure

'The executioner can come back tomorrow,' says King Shahriyar. 'My wife's finishing the story of Duban the Doctor tonight.'

That night – with Shahriyar and Dunyazid to hear her – Sheherazade goes on with her story:

word a thing that you say or write

page this book has fifty-one pages

One day, King Yunan says to his Vizier, 'You're right. Duban wants to kill me. What must I do?'

'Cut off his head,' says the Vizier, darkly.

Yunan's men bring Duban to him at once.

'You want to kill me, so I must kill you first,' cries the King.

'You're wrong! I'm your friend, Yunan,' answers the doctor.

But the King cries, 'Call the executioner!'

Then Duban says, 'Wait! Today I want to say goodbye to my friends and to give away all my things. Can you please kill me tomorrow?'

'All right,' says Yunan.

*The next day, Duban gives an old book to the King and says, 'Here's a wonderful present for you. Once I'm dead, put my head by you and read the **words** on **page** three of this book to it. Then, when you ask my dead head any question, it must answer.'*

After that, the executioner cuts off the doctor's head.

At once, Yunan puts Duban's head by him and looks for page three in the book. But something stops the pages opening. The King **licks** his **finger** and opens the book at page one, but there's nothing to read. He licks his finger again, and opens the book at page two. Again, there's nothing to read. He licks his finger once more, and opens the book at page three. It's a white page, too.

lick to put water from your mouth on something with your tongue

finger you have five of these on your hand

'There's nothing in this book!' cries King Yunan, angrily. But he's wrong; there's poison on its pages, on his finger, and in his mouth – and it soon kills him.

'So Duban kills Yunan after Yunan kills him,' cries Shahriyar. 'Truly you can never trust your friends.'

'You can't trust bad men,' says Sheherazade, 'but you can – and must – trust your true helpers. Would you like to hear a new story? The night is young.'

'Yes,' says Shahriyar.

'Please,' says Dunyazid. So Sheherazade begins:

poor without much money

courtyard a place in the middle of a house that is open to the sky

dream pictures that you see in your head when you are sleeping

treasure something expensive, like gold or jewels

mosque Muslims go here to pray

In Baghdad, in the days of Haroun al-Rashid, a **poor** man lives in a poor house with two tall trees at the front, and a little black and white pool in the **courtyard**. One night, he has a **dream**. In it a man tells him, 'Go to Cairo. You can find **treasure** there.'

So the poor man goes to Cairo. But – with no friends there, and no money for a room – where can he stay? In the end, he sleeps in the courtyard of a **mosque**. That night, near the mosque, some bad men go through the window of a rich man's house. They want to take all his money. But the rich man hears them, and comes after them. So they run away.

Then the rich man sees the man from
Baghdad in the mosque courtyard and thinks,
'That's one of them!' So he calls the **Chief of Police** and his
men. They arrive, hit the poor man with big sticks, and take him
half-dead to **prison**.

The next day, the Chief of Police asks him, 'Where are you
from? And why are you here?'

Just then, the Vizier arrives from the courtyard. It is
morning, and again the executioner is waiting.

Chief of Police
the most
important man in
a town who stops
people from doing
bad things

prison a place
where people
must stay when
they do something
wrong

READING CHECK

Are these sentences true or false? Tick the boxes.

		True	False
a	'The Vizier wants to kill me,' King Yunan thinks one day.	☐	☐
b	King Yunan wants to kill Duban before Duban kills him.	☐	☐
c	The next day, Duban gives the king a new book.	☐	☐
d	'Read the words on page three to my head,' he says.	☐	☐
e	The executioner cuts off Duban's hands.	☐	☐
f	King Yunan opens the book, but he can't open page three.	☐	☐
g	He licks his fingers and opens the pages of the book.	☐	☐
h	There's poison on the pages and he soon dies.	☐	☐
i	Sheherazade's next story is about a rich man from Baghdad.	☐	☐
j	One night, he has a dream about some treasure in Baghdad.	☐	☐
k	He goes to Cairo and lots of good things happen to him there.	☐	☐

WORD WORK

Use the pictures to write sentences with words from Chapter 4.

a Look at the picture on one.

...Look at the picture on page one...................................

b Can you put your 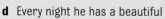 here, please?

....

c When it's hot, we often eat in the .

....

d Every night he has a beautiful ....

....

e There's in the old man's garden, people say.

....

f Now that carefully. You don't want it all over your face.

....

g There's a big near my house.

....

h The police want to take the man to .

....

GUESS WHAT

What happens in the next chapter? Tick the boxes.

a The Chief of Police tells the poor man, ...
- ☐ 'Go back to Baghdad!'
- ☐ 'There's some treasure in the king's palace.'
- ☐ 'You must give a present to the king.'

b The poor man from Baghdad finds some treasure ...
- ☐ in prison.
- ☐ near the mosque in Cairo.
- ☐ in the courtyard of his house.

c When Sheherazade finishes the story, Shahriyar ...
- ☐ is sleeping.
- ☐ wants to hear a new story.
- ☐ calls for the executioner.

~ CHAPTER 5 ~
The black wooden horse

'I need my wife for one more night, Vizier,' says Shahriyar. 'She's finishing the story "Dreams of far-away treasure" this evening. The executioner can have her tomorrow.'

That night, Sheherazade goes on with her story, and Shahriyar and Dunyazid listen happily:

crazy not thinking well

dig to take away earth

So the Chief of Police questions the poor man, and he says, 'I'm from Baghdad, and I'm looking for treasure here in Cairo.' And he tells the Chief of Police about his dream.

*'You're **crazy**,' cries the Chief of Police. 'Go back to Baghdad this minute. There's no treasure here.'*

'But in my dream, I remember...' begins the man from Baghdad.

*'Forget it. I too have a dream sometimes where a man speaks to me of treasure. He tells me, "Go to Baghdad to a poor house with two tall trees at the front, and a little black and white pool in the courtyard. **Dig** under the pool, and there you can find lots of treasure."*

'But do I go to
Baghdad?' laughs
the Chief of Police. 'No,
I don't. Because it's only a
dream, my crazy friend, nothing
more. I stay here in Cairo. And so you must
go back to Baghdad and stay there.'

With that, the Chief of Police opens the prison door,
gives some money to the poor man, and says, 'You can go.'

So the poor man goes home to Baghdad. When he arrives, he
digs under the pool in his courtyard, finds lots of treasure there,
and is a rich and happy man for many years.

'What a crazy story!' laughs Shahriyar.

'Crazy, but true,' answers Sheherazade. 'Sometimes we don't find things when we *want* them, but when we *need* them. Would you like to hear a new story? We have time.'

'Of course,' answers Shahriyar.

'Let's,' says Dunyazid.

So Sheherazade begins:

In Old Persia at New Year, people give presents to the King. One year, an old man from India comes to the palace with a big, black, **wooden** horse.

'This wonderful present is for you,' he tells King Sabur.

'A wooden horse isn't very wonderful,' answers the King.

'Ah, but it can **fly**. Watch!' And with that, the old Indian gets on the horse's back, and moves its left **ear**. At once, the horse flies up to the sky.

When the old man comes back down and gets off the horse's back, King Sabur asks him, 'How much do you want for this wonderful horse?'

wooden made of wood

fly to go through the air

ear you have two of these on your head, and you hear with them

'I don't want money, my King. I want to marry your youngest daughter.'

'Never!' cries the King's son, **Prince** Firouz.

But King Sabur is very interested in the wooden horse.

'Son,' he says, 'please look at that horse carefully before you answer this man.'

So Firouz goes to the horse and gets on its back.

'My Prince,' begins the Indian. 'When you want to fly up, you move the horse's left ear—'

'I know,' says the Prince angrily. He moves the horse's left ear, and it flies up into the sky and doesn't come back.

'Where's my son?' asks the King after some time.

'I don't know,' cries the Indian. 'I had no time to tell him about when he wants to come down again.'

'Take this man to prison!' says the King angrily. 'And call the executioner at once!'

Just then, the Vizier arrives.

'The executioner's here for Sheherazade,' he says.

prince the son of a king

READING CHECK

Choose the right words to finish the sentences.

a The poor man tells the Chief of Police in Cairo about …
   1 ☐ some treasure in Baghdad.
   2 ☑ his dream.
   3 ☐ the bad men in the rich man's house.

b The Chief of Police in Cairo tells the poor man, …
   1 ☐ 'I too sometimes have a dream.'
   2 ☐ 'You must stay in prison.'
   3 ☐ 'You must look for your treasure in Cairo.'

c Sheherazade begins a new story about …
   1 ☐ a white horse.
   2 ☐ an Indian king.
   3 ☐ an old man from India.

d The wooden horse flies when the old man …
   1 ☐ moves its head.
   2 ☐ moves its left ear.
   3 ☐ speaks to it.

e The king wants to give … to the old man for his wonderful horse.
   1 ☐ some money
   2 ☐ his youngest daughter
   3 ☐ a palace

f Prince Firouz gets on the horse and …
   1 ☐ goes to the palace.
   2 ☐ sees a beautiful woman.
   3 ☐ flies away.

g Prince Firouz can't …
   1 ☐ come back down.
   2 ☐ fly.
   3 ☐ go up in the sky.

h The king is … the old man.
   1 ☐ happy with
   2 ☐ angry with
   3 ☐ interested in

WORD WORK

1 Find words from Chapter 5 in the pools.

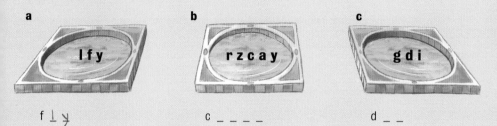

a

l f y

f l y

b

r z c a y

c _ _ _ _

c

g d i

d _ _

d

d o n o w e

w _ _ _ _ _

e

c r i n e p

p _ _ _ _ _

2 Use words from Activity 1 to complete the sentences.

a An old woman .. dig .. s under a tree and finds some treasure.

b That old man can't think very well. He's ....

c The young man over there is a .... His father is the king.

d In my dreams I can .... in the sky.

e The Indian's horse isn't alive; it's ....

GUESS WHAT

What happens in the next chapter? Tick three boxes.

a Shahriyar wants to hear more about the wooden horse. ☐

b Prince Firouz flies on the horse for years and years. ☐

c The old man from India marries a princess. ☐

d The King of Kashmir cuts off the old Indian's head. ☐

e Prince Firouz marries a beautiful princess. ☐

f The executioner kills Sheherazade after a thousand and one nights. ☐

~ CHAPTER 6 ~
Love and trust

land to arrive from the air; to come down to the floor

princess the daughter of a king

'Vizier,' says Shahriyar, 'I want to hear more about a wonderful black wooden horse. "Tomorrow", please tell the executioner.'

That night, with Dunyazid and Shahriyar to listen, Sheherazade goes on with her story:

Up on the wooden horse, Prince Firouz wants to come down. But when he moves the horse's left ear back, the horse goes up; when he moves it to the front, the horse goes fast across the evening sky.

Later he learns more. When he moves the horse's right ear back, the horse goes quickly back across the sky; when he moves it to the front, the horse goes down.

It is night when Prince Firouz brings the horse down from the sky. Which country is he in? He doesn't know. He **lands** on a big palace, gets off the horse, and goes down some stairs. He arrives in a big room. There on the bed is a beautiful **princess**, the daughter of the King of Bengal. She opens her eyes and sits up. Firouz sits by her and tells her his story.

That night, Firouz and the princess **fall in love**.

'Would you like to fly to Persia with me?' he asks.

'Yes,' she answers.

Early the next morning, they get on the wooden horse and fly to Persia.

Firouz leaves the princess with the horse in a little palace in the country.

'Wait here. I must tell my father about you. Then I can take you to him.'

So Firouz goes to his father. King Sabur is very happy to see him. 'Take word to the prison,' he tells one of his men. 'The Indian can go.'

But the old Indian hears about Prince Firouz and the Princess of Bengal, and he goes to the palace in the country.

'I come from Prince Firouz,' he tells the princess. 'We must fly now to King Sabur's palace on the wooden horse.'

fall in love to begin loving

The princess gets up happily behind the Indian. But they fly away to Kashmir, because the King there wants a wife. 'Perhaps I can give this woman to the King of Kashmir for lots of money!' thinks the old man.

The horse lands near the King's palace, and the Indian and the princess get off.

'Help!' she cries at once.

The King of Kashmir arrives on a white horse. He's hunting with his friends and the Indian doesn't know him.

'Who are you?' the King asks. 'And who's this woman?'

'I'm an old man from India and she's my young wife,' comes the answer.

'That's not true,' cries the princess, and she quickly tells the King everything.

'Right,' says the King and at once he cuts off the old Indian's head with his sword.

Then he takes the wooden horse and the princess back home to his palace.

clothes people wear these

'Marry me!' he cries once they are there.

What can the princess do? She begins to cry and laugh, and to say crazy things.

'She's crazy!' thinks the King of Kashmir. 'I can't marry a crazy woman. I must find a cure for her.'

Many doctors come and give medicine to the princess, but she stays crazy.

In Persia, Prince Firouz hears about the crazy Princess of Bengal, and her black wooden horse in the palace in Kashmir. He puts on doctor's **clothes** and goes there at once.

'I'm a Persian doctor. I can cure the princess,' he tells the King, 'So bring her here. And the black wooden horse is making her crazy, so I need that, too.'

'Of course, Doctor,' says the King, and his men bring the horse and the princess to him.

Then the Prince of Persia quietly tells the princess, 'Under these doctor's clothes it's me, Firouz. Trust me.'

'I do,' she answers quietly.

Suddenly, the prince takes her in his arms, gets on the wooden horse, and quickly flies away to Persia. Once there, they marry and live happily for many years, and have many sons and daughters.

For a thousand and one nights, Sheherazade tells stories to King Shahriyar – of Aladdin, Ali Baba, Sinbad, and more. And in that time Sheherazade and Shahriyar have three sons.

One morning, Sheherazade brings them to the King and says, 'I have no more stories to tell. Please don't kill me. Truly, I love our sons more than any mother can. **Spare** me, my **husband**.'

'I spare you happily!' says Shahriyar. 'Because you're a good mother and wife, and a wonderful teller of stories – and because I love and trust you, too, Sheherazade. Your cure works: I'm angry with women no longer! I can **forgive** them. I thank you for that.'

Later, Shahriyar gives the good **news** to his Vizier, Sheherazade's father, and the Vizier happily tells everyone in the country.

When Shahzaman hears the news, he visits his brother at once. He meets Sheherazade's sister, Dunyazid, on this visit, and he marries her soon after that.

So Shahriyar and Sheherazade, and Shahzaman and Dunyazid, live happily for many years. And they have many tall sons and beautiful daughters between them.

spare not to kill
husband the man that a woman marries
forgive to stop being angry with someone after they do something bad
news when someone tells you something that is new

READING CHECK

Put these sentences in the correct order. Number them 1–10.

a ☐ The Indian flies away to Kashmir with the princess.

b ☐ Prince Firouz and the Princess of Bengal fall in love.

c ☐ The princess says crazy things because she doesn't want to marry the king.

d ☐ Prince Firouz lands on a big palace in Bengal and gets off the horse.

e ☐ The King of Kashmir cuts off the Indian's head.

f ☐ Firouz and the princess fly from Kashmir to Persia on the horse.

g ☐ Firouz and the princess fly from Bengal to Persia on the horse.

h ☐ The King of Kashmir wants to marry the Princess of Bengal.

i ☐ Firouz puts on some doctor's clothes and goes to Kashmir.

j ☐ The old Indian hears about the Princess of Bengal and goes to her.

WORD WORK

1 Find eight more words from Chapter 6 in the wordsquare.

f	a	l	l	i	n	l	o	v	e
o	x	a	p	g	e	h	u	w	j
r	k	n	o	z	w	v	n	e	k
g	u	d	q	b	s	s	y	k	c
i	s	y	j	x	q	p	l	r	l
v	g	h	u	s	b	a	n	d	o
e	a	r	j	d	v	r	n	s	t
d	n	e	b	i	l	e	h	d	h
k	p	r	i	n	c	e	s	s	e
c	t	n	a	h	c	h	e	k	s

2 **Use the words from Activity 1 in the correct form to complete the sentences.**

a We're ... *landing* ... in Istanbul airport at 12.50.

b .... Noor of Jordan is a beautiful woman.

c Romeo .... with Juliet when they meet at her father's house.

d Why do you always wear black .... ?

e Please don't kill my children – .... them!

f Barack Obama is Michelle Obama's ....

g 'You're very late!' 'I'm sorry. .... me!'

h What are you doing these days? Tell me all your ....

i I can't hear you very well. My .... have got water in them.

WHAT NEXT?

1 **Here are more of Sheherazade's stories. Match the names with the story summaries. Use a dictionary to help you.**

a ☐   b ☐   c ☐

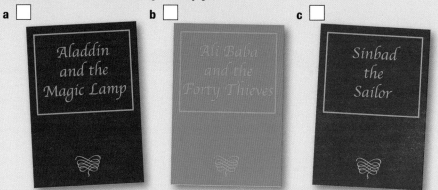

1 A poor man visits many different countries across the seas. He has many adventures and sails back to Baghdad a rich and happy man in the end.

2 A poor boy finds a wonderful lamp. With its magic to help, he is soon rich, has a palace to live in, and marries a princess. But what happens when he loses the lamp?

3 A poor man finds some robbers' treasure. He takes some of it, but the forty robbers come to find him and kill him. How can his servant girl Morgiana stop them?

2 **Which of these stories do you know? Which would you like to read? Why?**

Project A   *Telling a story*

1   Circle the correct words and phrases to complete the story of *The Little Beggar*.

a   *One / That* evening, a tailor and his wife meet a little beggar and he goes home with them.

b   They are eating fish and *after that / suddenly* the beggar gets a fish bone in his throat and stops moving.

c   *Suddenly / So* the tailor puts the beggar in a blanket, takes him to a doctor's house and asks for the doctor.

d   One minute *after / later*, the doctor runs down the stairs, sees the beggar and thinks, 'I'm his killer!'

e   *After that / After*, the doctor and his wife put the beggar in their neighbour's kitchen.

f   *Then / When* the cook comes home, he sees the beggar in the kitchen.

g   *After / Later*, the cook puts the beggar in the street, a rich man hits him.

h   *When / Then* a watchman comes and takes the rich man to the judge.

i   *Just then / So*, the fish bone falls out of the beggar's mouth and he sits up.

j   *Suddenly / In the end*, the little beggar goes to live at the palace with the king.

2 Read and order the story of Ali Baba.

a ☐ They go to Ali Baba's house and they wait in big oil jars in the garden.

b ☐ Soon Ali Baba's brother learns about the treasure and goes to the cave.

c ☐ In the end, Ali Baba lives happily with the treasure for many years.

d ☐ So he goes after the men, and he sees them go into a treasure cave.

e ☐ After this, the bad men want to kill Ali Baba.

f ☐ When the men go away, Ali Baba takes some treasure from the cave.

g ☐ Suddenly, the bad men arrive at the cave and kill the brother.

h ☐ One day, Ali Baba hears some bad men. They're talking about treasure.

i ☐ Some time later, Ali Baba takes his brother's dead body from the cave.

j ☐ Just then, a girl in the house hears the men and kills them with hot oil.

3 Choose a red title and write a story. Use the blue phrases to help you.

> *The bad wife/The two sisters/The father and his son*
>
> *One day ...*　　　*So ...*　　　*Soon ...*
>
> *Suddenly ...*　*When ...*　　　*After this ...*
>
> *Some time later ...*
>
> *Just then ...*　　　　　*In the end ...*

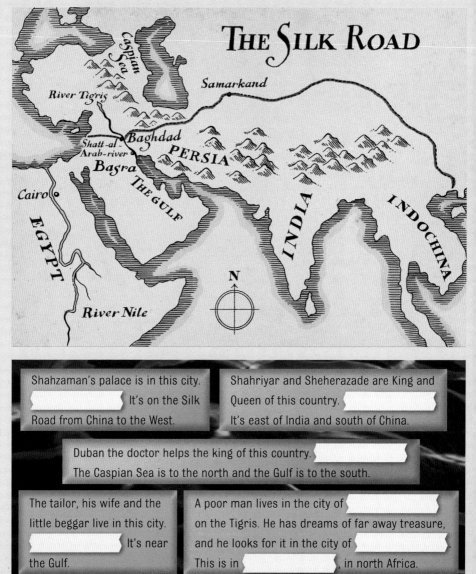

Project B *Places from stories*

1 **Look at the map of some of the places in the story of *Sheherazade*.**
   Read and write the place names.

Shahzaman's palace is in this city.
_____ It's on the Silk
Road from China to the West.

Shahriyar and Sheherazade are King and
Queen of this country. _____
It's east of India and south of China.

Duban the doctor helps the king of this country. _____
The Caspian Sea is to the north and the Gulf is to the south.

The tailor, his wife and the
little beggar live in this city.
_____ It's near
the Gulf.

A poor man lives in the city of _____
on the Tigris. He has dreams of far away treasure,
and he looks for it in the city of _____
This is in _____, in north Africa.

2 Look up the words in the box in a dictionary. Then read and complete.

buildings	canals	capital	country	city
peninsula	port	region	river	world

Samarkand is a big _____ in Uzbekistan in Central Asia. It's over 2,750 years old and there are many old Islamic _____ there.

Today we call Persia 'Iran'. It's a big _____ in the Middle East near Central and South Asia. It's one of the oldest countries in the _____. Most Iranians are Muslims and they speak Farsi.

Tehran

IRAN

Basra is in the south of Iraq. It's the third biggest city in the country and it's an important _____. The city is next to the Shatt al-Arab river, and there are many little _____ there.

Indochina is a _____ in Southeast Asia. It's on a _____ east of India and south of China. Today the countries in Indochina are Cambodia, Laos and Vietnam.

INDOCHINA

Cairo is the _____ of Egypt. It has many mosques, so people sometimes call it 'the city of a thousand minarets'. It's on the _____ Nile and is near the pyramids and the Great Sphinx in Giza.

3 Match the places with the stories.

a Lake Lucerne

b La Mancha

c Sherwood Forest

d The Arabian Desert

1 Layla and Majnun live in tents in …

2 Robin Hood lives under the trees in …

3 Don Quixote comes from a village in …

4 William Tell and his son live in a house near …

4 Choose a story place. Find out some information about it and complete the table.

Story title:	
Place name:	
What happens here in the story?	
Where is it?	
Description:	
What can you do here today?	

GRAMMAR

GRAMMAR CHECK

Short answers

We use short answers to reply to Yes/No questions. In a short answer, we re-use the auxiliary verb or the verb *be* from the question. The pronoun in the answer matches the subject of the question.

Is Shahzaman the King of Samarkand? Yes, he is.

We use the same pronoun in the short answer as in the question.

Does he go back to his room for his brother's present? Yes, he does.

1 **Write short answers for these questions about Shahzaman and Shahriyar.**

a Does Shahzaman find his wife in his room with her sister?

..No, he doesn't...

b Does he find her there with a young man?...........................

c Can Shahzaman trust his wife after this?...........................

d Is he angry with her?

....

e Does he spare her?

....

f Are Shahzaman and Shahriyar brothers?...........................

g Do the two of them live in Samarkand?...........................

h Is Shazaman smiling when he gives his present to Shahriyar?...........................

i Can Shahzaman see Shahriyar's wife from the window of his room?

....

j Is she with her women and some palace servants?...........................

k Are they in the pool?...........................

l Is Shahriyar's wife better than Shahzaman's wife?...........................

m Do Shahzaman and Shahriyar talk that night?...........................

n Does Shahriyar's wife want Masood to be king after her husband dies?

....

o Does Shahriyar's wife say sorry to her husband before she dies?

....

GRAMMAR CHECK

Comparative adjectives

We add –er to make the comparative form of most adjectives.	*old – older* *quiet – quieter*
When adjectives finish in e, we add –r.	*nice – nicer*
When adjectives finish in consonant + y, we change y to i and add –er.	*angry – angrier*
When adjectives finish in a short vowel and a single consonant, we double the consonant and add –er.	*big – bigger*
With longer adjectives (other 2 syllable adjectives, or adjectives with 3+ syllables) we use more.	*beautiful – more beautiful*
Some adjectives have an irregular comparative form.	*bad – worse* *good – better*

2 **Write comparative sentences about Sheherazade and Dunyazid.**

a Dunyazid/young/Sheherazade

.. Dunyazid is younger than Sheherazade ....

b Dunyazid/afraid/Sheherazade ....

c Sheherazade/tall/Dunyazid ....

d Sheherazade/beautiful/Dunyazid ....

e Dunyazid/quiet/Sheherazade ....

f Sheherazade/interesting/Dunyazid ....

g Dunyazid/excited/Sheherazade ....

h Dunyazid/careful/Sheherazade ....

3 **Write comparative sentences about Sheherazade and Shahriyar with these adjectives.**

a old .Shahriyar is older than Sheherazade ...

b angry ....

c nice ....

d bad ....

e big ....

f good ....

GRAMMAR

GRAMMAR CHECK

Information questions and question words

We use question words to ask information questions.

We answer these questions by giving information.

Where does Shahzaman live?

In his palace in Samarkand.

Why does Shahzaman cut off his wife's head?

Because he can't trust her any more.

What's the name of Shahzaman's first wife?

We don't know.

4 Complete the information questions with the question words in the box.

How	How many	How much	What	When
Where	Which	~~Who~~	Who	Why

a Q: ......Who...... is Sheherazade's father?

A: King Shahriyar's Vizier.

b Q: .... daughters does he have?

A: Two.

c Q: .... are their names?

A: Sheherazade and Dunyazid.

d Q: .... does the Vizier help King Shahriyar?

A: He finds a new wife for him every day.

e Q: .... doesn't the Vizier feel happy when he comes home one night?

A: Because he can't find any more wives for the king.

f Q: .... of his daughters marries King Shahriyar?

A: Sheherazade.

g Q: .... does Sheherazade tell stories to her husband?

A: In the king's room.

h Q: .... listens to the stories with Shahriyar?

A: Sheherazade's sister, Dunyazid.

i Q: .... does Sheherazade love her three sons?

A: More than any mother can.

j Q: .... does Shahzaman marry Dunyazid?

A: Soon after he meets her on a visit to his brother's palace.

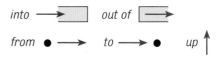

GRAMMAR

GRAMMAR CHECK

Prepositions and prepositional verbs

We use prepositions of place to say where things are.

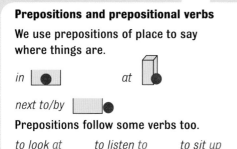

in | *at*

next to/by

Prepositions of movement tell us how something moves.

into | *out of*

from | *to* | *up*

Prepositions follow some verbs too.

to look at   *to listen to*   *to sit up*

---

5 Circle the correct prepositions to complete the sentences about the story *The Little Beggar*.

a The story happens *in / by* Baghdad.

b The tailor and his wife take the little beggar *to / at* their house.

c When the little beggar gets a fish bone *into / in* his throat, he falls *out of / from* the table.

d After the tailor and his wife put the beggar *in / to* a blanket, they take him *into / at* the street.

e They take him *to / from* the doctor's house, and they leave him *in / at* the foot of the stairs.

f After the doctor knocks over the little beggar, he looks *to / at* the body carefully.

g The doctor and his wife leave the little beggar *to / in* the cook's kitchen.

h The cook takes things to eat *to / from* the palace every night.

i The cook leaves the little beggar *by / in* a shop.

j The rich man suddenly sees the little beggar *next to / at* him.

k 'This man wants to take my money *out of / from* me,' the rich man cries.

l When the rich man hits the little beggar, the beggar's body falls *in / at* his feet.

m People come *up / out of* their houses and listen *to / at* the judge.

n After the fish bone falls *into / out of* the little beggar's mouth, he sits *in / up*.

GRAMMAR CHECK

Modal auxiliary verbs: can and can't

We use can + the infinitive without *to* to talk about things we are able to do.

King Yunan can play polo.

We use can't + the infinitive without *to* for things we are not able to do.

The doctors in Persia can't cure King Yunan's leprosy.

We don't use do/does in questions with can.

Can Duban help the king?

6 Complete the sentences about the story *Duban the Doctor* with the verbs in the box.

can be   ~~can cure~~   can get up   can go   can…kill   can kill   can't open   can put
can't read   can say   can't see   can sit   can't stop   can…trust   can't trust

a 'I ..*can cure*.. you differently from the doctors here,' says Duban.

b 'Do that, and you .... rich,' says Yunan.

c 'The medicine in this polo stick .... through your skin and cure you,' says Duban.

d 'Tomorrow you .... a well man,' he finishes.

e After Duban cures Yunan, he .... by the king.

f 'When a man .... medicine in a polo stick, he .... you with poison too,' says Yunan's vizier.

g Soon Yunan .... Duban any more, and he wants to kill him.

h Duban talks to his old friend Yunan, but he .... the king.

i '................. you .... me tomorrow?' he asks.

j Duban .... goodbye to his friends.

k Yunan takes Duban's book in his hands, but he .... its pages very easily.

l Yunan .... any words on page three.

m He .... the white poison on the white pages.

n .... kings .... their friends or not?

GRAMMAR CHECK

Linkers: *so* and *because*

We use **so** to link two sentences when the second sentence explains a result.

A man from Baghdad dreams about treasure in Cairo <u>so he goes there</u>.

result of first part of sentence

We use **because** to link two sentences when the second sentence explains a reason.

He's interested in treasure <u>because he's very poor</u>.

reason for first part of sentence

7 **Complete the sentences about the story *Dreams of Far-Away Treasure* with *so* or *because*.**

a In Cairo, the poor man sleeps in the courtyard of a mosque ...*because*... he has no money for a room.

b Some bad men want money .... they go through the window of a rich man's house one night.

c The rich man gets up at night .... he hears a noise in the night.

d The rich man goes after the bad men .... they all run away.

e The rich man sees the poor man near his house .... he thinks, 'That's one of them!'

f The Chief of Police and his men arrive .... the rich man calls them.

g They hit the poor man with sticks .... they're angry with him.

h Bad men must go to prison .... they take the poor man there.

i The Chief of Police asks, 'Where are you from and why are you here?' .... the poor man tells him about his dream of treasure in Cairo.

j The poor man goes back to Baghdad .... the Chief of Police tells him about his dream of treasure there.

k The Chief of Police gives the poor man some money when he leaves .... he feels sorry for him.

l The poor man remembers the Chief of Police's words .... he digs under the pool in his courtyard.

m In the end, the man from Baghdad is happy .... he is rich.

GRAMMAR

GRAMMAR CHECK

Position of adjectives

When we use a number of adjectives before a noun we put them in this order:

article	feeling, appearance, value	size	age	colour	material, place, nationality	noun
a	wonderful	big	new	black	wooden	horse

8 **Complete the sentences about the story** *The Black Wooden Horse* **with the words in brackets in the correct order.**

a Sabur is a ..happy..old..Persian... king. (Persian/old/happy)

b He lives in a .... palace. (wonderful/old/big)

c On New Year's Day an .... man arrives. (Indian/interesting/old)

d He gives a/an .... present to the King. (new/exciting/wooden)

e Firouz is a .... prince. (rich/Persian/young)

f He arrives in Bengal one .... night. (Arabian/warm/dark)

g He finds a .... princess in her room. (young/Bengali/beautiful)

h He takes her to a .... palace and goes to his father. (country/little/nice)

i The Indian leaves his .... room and finds the princess. (dark/cold/prison)

j He takes the princess to a .... garden in Kashmir. (green/nice/big)

k The King of Kashmir arrives on a .... horse. (white/tall/Arabian)

l He cuts off the Indian's head with a/an .... sword. (Syrian/expensive/new)

m The King of Kashmir doesn't want a .... wife. (Bengali/young/crazy)

n A/An .... doctor comes and speaks to him. (old/Persian/good)

DOMINOES
THE STRUCTURED APPROACH TO READING IN ENGLISH

Dominoes is an enjoyable series of illustrated classic and modern stories in four carefully graded language stages – from Starter to Three – which take learners from beginner to intermediate level.

Each *Domino* reader includes:
- **a good story** to read and enjoy
- **integrated activities** to develop reading skills and increase active vocabulary
- **personalized projects** to make the language and story themes more meaningful
- **seven pages of grammar activities** for consolidation.

Each *Domino* pack contains a reader, plus a MultiROM with:
- **a complete audio recording of the story,** fully dramatized to bring it to life
- **interactive activities** to offer further practice in reading and language skills and to consolidate learning.

If you liked this Starter Level *Domino*, why not read these?

Mulan
Janet Hardy-Gould

When the Emperor calls every man to join the army and fight the enemy, Mulan's father is old and ill, and cannot go. Wearing men's clothes and riding a horse, Mulan leaves her family and fights bravely for the Emperor in her father's place.

She is soon a hero for all the soldiers in the Chinese army. One of them, Ye Ming, is her best friend. But does he know that she is a woman? And can Mulan fall in love with a friend?

Book ISBN: 978 0 19 424706 1
MultiROM Pack ISBN: 978 0 19 424670 5

Heidi
Johanna Spyri

'I'm not going with you, Aunt Dete!' Heidi cries.
'Oh yes, you are!' Dete answers.

Heidi loves her home in the Swiss mountains, her grandfather, and her friend Peter, the goatherd. So when Aunt Dete takes her away to Frankfurt, she doesn't leave happily.

In Frankfurt, Heidi is soon good friends with Clara Sesemann, a rich but very ill girl in a wheelchair. But how can Heidi live without the mountains? And what can she do about Fräulein Rottenmeier, the Sesemanns' unfriendly housekeeper?

Book ISBN: 978 0 19 424913 3
MultiROM Pack ISBN: 978 0 19 424911 9

You can find details and a full list of books in the *Dominoes* catalogue and Oxford English Language Teaching Catalogue, and on the website: www.oup.com/elt

Teachers: see www.oup.com/elt for a full range of online support, or consult your local office.

	CEF	Cambridge Exams	IELTS	TOEFL iBT	TOEIC
Starter	A1	YLE Movers	–	–	–
Level 1	A1–A2	YLE Flyers/KET	3.0	–	–
Level 2	A2–B1	KET-PET	3.0-4.0	–	–
Level 3	B1	PET	4.0	57-86	550